"Flat-out brilliant. Its wit and intell
Smooth taffy enjambments pull th
figurations of meaning into the ne
enthusiasm. At the same time, deftly ....
the lineal interiors. Throughout this long poem, seemingly familiar
diction and grammar comes spiked with word substitutions so startling,
they suspend our semantic links and subvert snatches of narrative. In
fact, the whole poem seems to be constructed on a tonal framework of
transilient melodic improvisations. And yet 'SestinaLA' is definitively a
philosophical poem concerned with the nature of identity and with the
proposition that 'it is impossible/ to distinguish one self from another.'
What makes the poem so exceptional is that its theme is developed
with such vivid formalism (since, as the poet writes, a 'thing is always
determined by its/ function') in shifting fields of music and language
where restless subjects shimmer into and out of view.'"

— FORREST GANDER, Judge's citation
for the Poetry Society of America's Cecil Hemley Memorial award

"Karla Kelsey's *Blood Feather* interrogates the lush terrain of identi-
ty and gender 'from the self-as-object to the self-as-process' in three
striking dramatic dialogs. As interested in expanding the possibilities
of the individual poem as she is in decomposing the construction of
our notions of the book as book (subtitles such as Part One, Part Two,
etc. appear throughout each monologue as we read on, each sending
us back to prior intervals in previous poems), Kelsey reveals a kaleido-
scopic view of how the feminine builds itself even as it contends with
received constraints of history and gesture. No wonder Maya Deren,
our great filmmaker, choreographer, dancer and poet makes a crucial
appearance at the end, she who said, 'In film I make the world dance.'
Kelsey's performance of the performance of female gender is ultimately
engaged in the act of being and the act of art—and their indelible,
magnificent relation. More theatre than book, in *Blood Feather*, once
one takes a bow, another movement begins. The work is on a continual
refresh."

—GILLIAN CONOLEY

"*Blood Feather*, like the body, as Simone de Beauvoir said, is not a thing, but a situation. In three gripping dramatic monologues, Karla Kelsey gloriously expands the literary genre of ekphrasis into the 'rips gaps revealing unmapped places where / beauty might take root.' The poet has built an exquisite overlay, a stunning performance of voices who reach widely and deeply into history, philosophy, art, literature, design, film, and music. In these propulsive poems about the female gaze, Kelsey affirms B.K. Fischer's argument that feminist ekphrasis 'comprises acts of description and interrogation, improvisation and analysis, homage and backtalk.' The first poem announces 'in autumn I decided / the cancel desire cancel Eve cancel / Venus,' and thus we step breathlessly into the swan boat of a young actress, who deviates from recited scripts of gender. Destabilizing Aristotle's truism, 'you come to exist as an object / when you are looked at,' she looks back, listens, and speaks. A brilliant woman, married to an architect, reflects upon personal, artistic, and planetary design in the second poem, revealing that any object's or creature's (even the Firebird's) vulnerability is essential to its flight. In it, a tenacious woman in a fluid red gala dress stands 'my spine feathering language into fire.' Our heroine collaborates with Maya Deren in the final poem, performing a woman possessed, as we, too, are haunted by a grand meditation upon the ethics of aesthetics, especially in times of war: 'destruction's a cause / for coming into being,' she reminds us. Handing us this 'glowing feather,' Kelsey inhabits lives corseted by received narratives, 'the texts of the world,' yet tatters and re-stitches their stories into a 'suit of light.'"

— Camille Guthrie

BLOOD FEATHER

BLOOD FEATHER

Karla Kelsey

TUPELO PRESS

North Adams, Massachusetts

Library of Congress Control Number: 2020942321.

ISBN-13: 978-1-946482-41-9

Cover image: Collage by Ashley Lamb. Used by permission.
Cover and text design by Ann Aspell.

First paperback edition October 2020

Tupelo Press
P.O. Box 1767
North Adams, Massachusetts 01247
(413) 664-9611 / Fax: (413) 664-9711
editor@tupelopress.org / www.tupelopress.org

Tupelo Press is an award-winning independent literary press that publishes
fine fiction, non-fiction, and poetry in books that are a joy to hold as well as
read. Tupelo Press is a registered 501(c)(3) non-profit organization, and we rely
on public support to carry out our mission of publishing extraordinary work
that may be outside the realm of the large commercial publishers. Financial
donations are welcome and are tax deductible.

CONTENTS

BLOOD FEATHER

THREE SPRIGS OF ROSEMARY BOUND WITH RED THREAD

"The person inside a literary creation can be both viewer
and insider. The window is open and the bird flies in.
It closes and a drama between the bird
and its environment begins."

BARBARA GUEST, "Shifting Persona"

ONE

[PART FIRST] in autumn I decided
to cancel desire cancel Eve cancel
Venus cancel elicit meetings with Hadley
under the park's coral-colored bandstand in
the rain because where did that
get anyone but looking at the

swan boats sadly and rain has
a way of showing costumes for
what they really are those diamonds
are rhinestones and my waist measures
17 inches because of pills shapewear
and cigarettes the absence of Mother

doesn't mean the absence of Mother's
voice murmuring *that season I was*
jonquils jonquils jonquils murmuring *though things*
have a way of turning out
so very badly you had a
most romantic birth in the bow

of a boat rocked to sleep
in a hammock bed next to
a miniature orange tree waiting for
a table at The Ivy I
practice my audition for *The Glass*
Menagerie ribbon in my hair soft

violet slip dress I nervously echo
a laugh twist my hands catch
my breath Hadley thought I was
just a child and this was
the crux of his fascination but
I'm not a child though it's

a fact I pretended to be
perched on his knee smothering his
face in tiny kisses making Lulu
eyes and biting my lower lip
when he unzipped his pants in
the car [PART SECOND] I once

played a cavewoman grunting and carving
the outline of a bull into
a brown plaster wall when the
season ended the figure followed me
appearing as Taurus in the sky
floating over the apple tree of

my desire tied horizontally along a
trellis something to rest my shoulder
against fruiting season extended by absorbing
the warmth of the building next
to you when Hadley asks where
I've been I practice Laura saying

most afternoons I've spent in the
jewel-box that big glasshouse where they
raise the tropical flowers as a

child visiting the park I always
begged to ride in a pink
swan my brother demanding the blue

and such disagreement would ensue that
before we unpacked our picnic Mother
would hurry us back to the
car in the absence of Hadley
the question of Hadley I loved
him—no—I never loved him

a truth that fails to unbalance
this wanting for I hold my
tongue to the pearl and say
battle say *I recite this script*
for you in a garden hidden
from Mother's view blue silk rose

pinned to her shoulder kohl etched
into lines around her eyes lipstick
seeping into the crannies of her
upper lip she tries and tries
and on some level I sympathize
[PART THIRD] I come upon myself

a lonely guilty thing as if
all one aspired to was a
glass body filled with milk and
mother-smells the pink frill of a
short frock scarlet bow lips kept
quiet oh how those minivan angels

their babies buckled into safety seats
envy me just look at this
tangle of thorns my nest cradled
deep in the crotch of such
a glorious tree he said *lips*
of red velvet teeth a lock

of pearl if your apples are
rotting right on the branch then
you might try three sprigs of
rosemary bound with red thread tuck
them between mattress and bedstead to
keep the house hot and animal

our park was modeled after the
Boston Commons funds were raised for
swan boats the town council opted
for pastel plastic two-seaters without painted
eyes blind birds circling at the
beach I practice a pause a

whisper of strings and the waves
break and the surfers surf [PART
FOURTH] at the therapist's I practice
Laura saying *he used to call*
me blue roses and the unicorn
stays on a shelf with some

horses that don't have horns but
all of them seem to get
along nicely together it was an

old high school prank sneaking into
the boathouse to give the swans
eyes I painted mine the red

of crawlspace of exit sign a
boy's hand on my ankle and
then moving up Sundays expose thoughts
for what they really are foil-backed
no light emitting from interior source
the mind a repository for heavy

solar mass I no more emptied
the apple of meaning than I
turned the swans to flesh and
feather and so pray oh pray
thou lake and sky come empty
me from the hotel's 32nd floor

I fling ropes of Swarovski crystals
I fling Vegas show tunes I
fly in my sequined dress my
suit of lights [PART FIFTH] call
me Andrine the life-sized Rubberdoll look
at me not a soulless silicone

creature but from flesh and blood
enclosed in a synthetic skin the
body doused in civet and ambergris
I practice entering saying *moon moon
moon* and so in the wane
of summer I swallowed his seed

by which I meant to grow
the tree internally exhaling apples to
sallow sky momentarily entranced by the
belief that the world would balance
had California only been an island
if only Mother had bathed her

infant in mineral springs if only
I had drunk from the fountain
of youth my blood would smell
of oranges born the same day
as João Rodrigues Cabrilho in truth
I was getting too old for

ruffled panties and garter flask strategic
lean against the wall back arched
tits out nose to the sky
but where do you go from
there I sat chain-smoking on the
bandstand stage when Hadley appeared and

as I squinted he became David
Bowie in a swan boat floating
operatic across the pond [PART SIXTH]
this is how we came to
wander the park renaming natural things
birds to boats trees to tinsel

thunder a scrap metal sheet and
though I had less I had
this sole lee had a table

for two had sex had crutch
my crux and when I fix
my eyes to near distance I

can create the illusion of thinking
but at what cost this revelation
for how far can you go
staring at weeds in the cracks
no true mother no father no
lover no-no-no traced into diamond-lines left

by a rail by a snail
for if you were born in this
town you were washed clean of
afterbirth by water diverted from someone
else's valley biting into the fruit
Hadley fastens his eyes on

distant lights upon such gestures I
have pinned the melting of polar
icecaps the percent of harvest lost
to fireblight and when he touched
my side and said *rib* before
even thinking I answered back *atom*

TWO

[PART FIRST] at the episode's end
we choose the pink swan and
paddle to the middle of the
lake thunderclouds massing camera pulling back
you can't hear our conversation but
my fluttering hands say *a mandolin*

moment my expression forms a terracotta
mask for when you perform a
character unsure the source of her
inner monologue you must prepare—you
may no longer be able to
distinguish the voice of one self

from that of another the photo
of Hadley squinting into sun making
him the sun my finger covers
half the lens this is the
way we become the oblivion of
skin haunted by the thought that

objects don't make possible our forms
of representation but rather representation makes
us as objects possible I've become
bored by the lounge chair umbrella
kiddy pool splashing nowhere to hide
but Ann Radcliffe's *Mysteries of Udolpho*

gothic landscape heroine I read the
close of day road winding into
a deep valley a vista opening
the darkest horrors of the east
our language becoming expressively complete only
when it embodies the subject-matter to

which we are devoted [PART SECOND]
I hold the language of river
rocks in my pocket next to
the language of the costume shop
corset Antoinette wig did I turn
you on more when I stripped

naked on the beach or when
I vanished gulls flocking klieg-lights at
each turn of the chase my
wheels skid closer to the cliff's
edge will I evade pursuit only
to fall in slow motion to

the ocean below *There* said Montoni
brooding from the pages of my
book *is* Udolpho across the patio
bordered by birds of paradise bougainvillea
trellises I gaze with melancholy awe
imagining a castle the moldering walls

of dark grey stone is it
me or a character repeatedly checking
her phone for messages checking thighs

stomach chest for the evenness of
her tan just consider the women
made possible by Aristotle's suggestion that

as we age we turn into
milk our inner fires extinguished in
thick pearly liquid Hadley posing against
the rusted-out hood of his car
whisky bottle half-empty face half-shaded by
the crushed brim of a cowboy

hat [PART THIRD] why such a
swagger pardner why such an exaggerated
drawl silent lonely and sublime Udolfo
stands sovereign frowning defiance on all
who dare invade its solitary reign
consider the monologue you create each

time you open your compact to
powder your nose touch-up your lips
touch-up your eyes in the second
act we both wear terracotta masks
we do it in the park
skirt pushed up back pressed against

a tree is it this character
or me who sleeps until noon
getting up to dress first in
the blue shot-silk blouse then T-shirt
halter top terrycloth robe the rest
of the day spent on the

couch wedged under the picture window
sun moving across the body across
the sky last night I dreamed
mother as Marie Antoinette hair in
a pouf sporting a little wooden
ship a dozen diamond fish [PART

FOURTH] on TV a woman demonstrates:
for *park* place the P hand-shape
on the upper side of the
chest for *part* slice the side
of one hand across the palm
of the other for *pallor* the

hand first pinches the cheek and
then opens up and moves down
to show blood leaving the face
breathing jonquils in the dark as
you identify with the ankh tattooed
at the small of your character's

back leather laced tight drivers looking
down from cabs at thighs at
Hadley's hand in mine I read
into twilight Udolpho's features deepening to
awful obscurity I gaze entranced until
its towers are the only thing

rising over the shadow of the
woods alone on the lake in
the park in my very own

boat I paddle halfway to shore
and find there is still halfway
to go and so I paddle

more yet I am still only
halfway there the boat becoming evermore
heavy how did it come to
be true that each distance traversed
is filled with ever-new distances communicated
in the language of obstacle walls

topped with razor wire alarm and
dog and security light [PART FIFTH]
a constellation was born when Hadley
pounded silver nails into the ceiling
calling *Taurus* calling *Charge* interior monologue
in a loop we choose the

living room for the penultimate scene
I'm in black he's behind the
camera I say *no* say *yes*
back of the hand to forehead
you are no Lillian Gish he
says I say *you are no*

father no lover he says *I'll*
send you back to Gardena with
a box of adders and wasps
in the beginning the idea of
Hadley had been entertaining getting it
on in his dark green Nova

in the rain and — after — writing
our names in the stars with
the cherries of our cigarettes but
now I am inside the play
inside the book my horse emerging
upon a heathy rock I've reached

the castle gates the deep tone
of the portal bell sounding *things
can only go badly from here*
when you perform a character obsessed
by the death of her daughter
sunhat apron-dress red beads wrapped around

her little wrist you find yourself
sitting in a café unable to
take your eyes off the little
girl whining at the table next
to you who wants to scoop
her up in your arms is

it your character is it you
[PART SIXTH] entering and exiting the
garden your character pauses at the
gate listening to the small mouths
she hears at the centers of
roses you hurry past bouquets at

the supermarket's entrance journey into the
desert to shed swimming pools swan
boats jonquils waiting until the woman

within should come open the wrought
iron gates I anxiously survey the
stone edifice but overspreading gloom allows

me to distinguish little more than
the rampart's massy walls the question
of Hadley now become a question
of land management—when fireblight's nearly
decimated the orchard should one burn
it to the ground or leave

it for aphid and codling moths
to devour the park now emptying
as sheets of water come down
and the question remains can the
swan be brought to shore before
it grows too heavy to paddle

THREE

[PART FIRST] a wet fate means
carry me off in rivers to
oceans means a plywood raft means
salt mixed with rust lets us
perform all that cannot be known
in a moment of vision the

actress learning the body if not
stimulated by inspiring impetus cannot respond
with enticing gestures moreover the audience
will feel this as under heat
of stage lights each motion slows
I take ten full seconds to

place my hand on your hand
you take ten full seconds to
turn away for according to the
Philosopher a thing is always determined
by its function an eye for
instance constituted by what it can

see and so I become the
apple tree before me leafless fruitless
a wet fate requires bailing out
water with a shoe by the
time I was twelve Mother was
whiling away her time teaching me

to darken the eyes pinken the
cheeks redden the lips for I
already aspired to the specific quality
of California light emanating over freeways
sprawl asphalt chaparral upwelling ocean [PART
SECOND] I drive out Sunset to

Pacific Coast Highway for Malibu hiking
into hills switchbacks scrub oak vistas
and the surprise always the surprise
of the Pacific the actress learns
whenever we work physically we find
things we never could find if

we did nothing but think Cleopatra
painting her lower lashline with malachite
paste shadowing eyelid to brow with
ground lapis lazuli *The Language of*
Hands tells us the fire hand
prone towards injury and accident is

long with short fingers tends to
have strong lines and whorl fingerprints
which catch on wind will we
listen when the Philosopher says *you*
come to exist as an object
when you are looked at when

I ask *will we listen* I
mean I I mean me for
some days I exist as if

existence meant posing naked on a
bearskin rug and some days I
exist as the first two seconds

ever caught on film playing in
a loop Roundhay garden 1888 dense
with lilac clutching at my dress
I turn around walking backwards your
coattails flying as you walk past
I turn around walking backwards your

coattails flying as you walk past
I turn around [PART THIRD] to
come into existence only when you
see yourself being seen in someone
else's face as in two characters
round the corner from opposite directions

first a formal expression of recognition
then the body registering the tug-pulse
of *I knew you when* hiking
through the yellows of mariposa lilies
monkey flowers bush poppy goldenrod ending
in hills upon hills charred by

last spring's extended wildfire to the
breath of Hadley softening under sleep
I surrender because if the boat
goes down I am of the
boat I am of the bottom
of the lake hair billowing with

eelgrass and small bubbles gently released
the actress learns therefore we're always
individually doing yoga we check our
breathing our posture our movement a
wet fate requiring notecards embossed with
waterlilies veins tributaries written in peacock

blue Egyptians knew kohl made of
lead oxidized copper ochre ash crushed
antimony burnt almonds lining the eyes
protects against infection and glare [PART
FOURTH] the jeweled eyes of Roman
women made-up with saffron ash date

stones charred roses glittering out from
behind the Lex Oppia law 215
BCE forbidding women to own more
than an ounce of gold ride
in carriages wear multicolored garments particularly
those trimmed in purple the moment

between waking and sleep taking us
further away from memory to enter
the weave of raw materials glass
unicorns plastic swan boats Hadley's lips
to my ear in a whisper
though the seeds release cyanide when

ingested it is not necessary to
core apples before giving them to
birds consider the function of the

hand as that of conducting—start
the birds start the engine start
the light stop the moon stop

the clock stop the heater in
its moan it was not the
ocean but a river explorers first
named for angels El Río de
Nuestra Señora la Reina de los
Ángeles de Porciúncula giving rise to

the pueblo Our Lady Queen of
the Angels later known as the
City of Flowers and Sunshine Tinseltown
LaLa Land in a burnt valley
where there once ran a small
river the actress learns the body's

awareness of what surrounds it a
necessity linking not only body and
food and body and sleep and
body and sex but the plastic
of the swan calling me to
the bottom of the lake [PART

FIFTH] Wagner's *Tristan* chord plays over
and over swelling the moon in
my body he says *I devour*
I say *I plunge* he says
I devour I say *I plunge*
he says *I devour* and I

say *what is necessarily is when*
it is and what is not
necessarily is not when it is
not applying white eyeliner to the
inner v of the eye adds
glimmer and freshness to the wearer's

gaze blue liner in the waterline
adds contrast rendering the whites of
the eyes even brighter the actress
learns there's hardly enough time to
practice life apply it to a
role the actress therefore learns emergency

images appear to us without conscious
willing her little boat caught in
a storm thunder crack rain aslant
her eyes gleam before she crests
over the waterfall I hike a
sharp incline silver manzanita burnt leafless

the panorama mountains volcanoes tapering blue
into ocean always ocean a wet
fate means casting about for pearls
and smooth whalebones means ashes scattered
out at sea for not everything
that *is* necessarily *is* and not

everything that *is not* necessarily *is*
not [PART SIXTH] the accumulation of
the present offset by the past

of rain boat park for if
I knew the weight of water
needed to sink this boat I

could calculate the very moment possibility
tips to inevitability making me a
seer catastrophic diving the water hand
long and rectangular tends to be
thin with many fine lines and
other marks I wake realizing I

had become a function of Hadley
leather jacket smelling of engine oil
gasoline animal rattling interior chains while
the self unknown inhabits the black
dress buoyant in wind arms working
through the sound of birds dubbed

in after the fact from this
height all that's left of the
west is a small ribbon of
cars traveling the highway and beyond
this: the Channel Islands and beyond
them: water meets air in near-invisible

horizon to become what shifts slowly
behind glass an accumulation of botanicals
animal fats sequins seashells rusted nails
buttons of pearl of seed as
dim sun mouths down I arrived
in a new faux fur cape

and hat with a netted veil
you knew me and you knew
me not for all that cannot
be realized in a moment of
perception locks within a retained image
that might or might not become

a reminder of love a mnemonic
of idea something touching us very
lightly like flower petals or a
kiss meditating upon this the actress
learns to want things yet unknown
to the controlled consciousness ruining us

FOUR

[PART FIRST] these were my reflections
as I stood before the lake
cradling a bargain bag of apples
in my arms three pounds of
symbolic desire nestling each apple's weight
in hand I name one *love*

I name one *sex* and I
name one *fame* establishing the fact
that another body's action is necessary
to cause a body to change
its state of motion a form
of beauty creating gaps in the

non-beautiful as in the new stage
adaptation of *Anna Karenina* along with
delivering Anna's lines I perform with
a little speaker in my ear
the director talks into it telling
me right on stage what I

have to say now *mirror* now
mercury now *silence* according to eternal
laws all that exists on this
earth must meet attract repulse kiss
and corrupt one another again and
again perhaps because of this the

starlet must learn to reject her
desire to ignore camera flash and
pointed question for while love can
resist familiarity eroticism cannot for example
in *The Judgment of Paris* each
goddess attempts to bribe Paris into

anointing her the fairest Hera promises
the thrones of Europe Minerva victory
in war Venus offers Helen the
daughter of Leda and the Swan
the most beautiful woman in the
world [PART SECOND] at the Malibu

Getty we view a particularly charming
depiction painted on a Kerch vase
circa 360 BCE Venus holds a
veil to her face in feigned
modesty the figures' colorful Asian attire
white skin and gold hair unique

to artifacts found in the Black
Sea colonies of ancient Greece cradling
each weight I anticipate the disruption
of the lake's placid surface oversized
handbags and glasses generate the image
of hidden spaces compelling us to

feel intimate with the starlet even
as she exists as an impossible
object shimmering before us in a

dress of violet silk for whatever
draws on or presses another is
as much drawn or pressed by

that other yet one of Hadley's
whispers never equals another whisper the
sound of arsenic in contrast with
the sound of fog the director
speaks intimacies never otherwise discussed right
into my ear I must immediately

repeat what he says regardless of
Vronsky exiting and Alexi Alexandrovich entering
regardless of sweeping dear little Seryozha
up in my arms [PART THIRD]
often instead of dialogue he poses
questions I answer directly turning now

to face the audience now back
to Levin then Kitty now bending
to whisper in Vronsky's ear from
the grand gesture of painted ceilings
to trifles such as engraved mirror
backings Italian inkstands wedding chests statuettes

Paris's judgment appears in illuminated manuscripts
and decorative art and from the
Middle Ages onwards all three goddesses
are presented nude when memory replays
as melodrama Hadley pulls the scarf
so tightly around my neck the

audience covers her eyes with her
hands peaks through small spaces between
fingers a silence poised before casting
each apple through air arc-back and
throw breaking water's surface into echo
of desire *love* after desire *sex*

after desire *fame* if a horse
draws a stone tied to a
rope the horse will be equally
drawn back towards the stone for
the body is a set of
possibilities to be continually realized even

in tell-all interviews the starlet preens
and confides but never reveals what
the actress is really like for
we adore an imaginary creature without
memory without a past retaining the
perfect innocence of a mythical child

in the accompanying photograph sun streams
through the modest lines of her
simple summer dress silhouetting full breasts
small waist and perfect ass [PART
FOURTH] cultivating herself as accessible legend
the starlet learns to enter the

ballroom matching satin gloves satin dress
kiss her director on the cheeks
right-left all while maintaining her signature

expression of dumbfounded delight the questions
become personal he asks me for
instance *Marina how are you dressed*

today or *tell me who you*
are Marina Marina try to discover
yourself try to describe yourself for
if a body impinge upon another
and change its motion the body
will also undergo an equal change

and thus we realize small points
rips gaps revealing unmapped places where
beauty might take root the occasion
for painting three female nudes proved
the scene particularly popular in the
Renaissance the subject rendered by Lucas

Cranach the Elder a full twenty-two
times the great Rubens returning to
the subject again and again in
repetition resides the pretty gesture with
which the neighbor girl drew the
blanket back from a kitten the

shape of its skull deformed with
enough repetition even a favorite word
lifts gold-leafed from its meaning as
if thought had the body of
an object I echo a rose
is a rose is a rose

but what are flowers made for
but the game of petals pulled
one and one and he loves
me he loves me not [PART
FIFTH] on more than one occasion
Hadley kept us at the farmer's

market far too long his hands
smoothing over ripe fruit before selecting
just one perfect apple to leave
rotting on the back seat of
his car the pleasure of looking
is rarely handed over to the

starlet except of course when it
might arouse the audience the apple
was unknown to the Near East
when the Temptation and Fall was
written scholars suppose the forbidden fruit
to more likely have been pomegranate

fig carob pear mushroom quince datura
almond the word *apple* a later
error of translation the Latin words
for *malum* evil and *mālum* apple
being nearly identical so I answer
him but at the same time

there is prepared dialogue ongoing and
I have to keep up with
this other narrative I have to

continue speaking Anna an essential piece
of any proper 19th-century academic artist's
portfolio *The Judgment* wanes in the

20th century although we have innovative
examples André Lhote's 1927 cubist painting
of two sailors admiring three bare-breasted
African women and in Venice I
saw Salvador Dali's lithograph three goddesses
shaped like Brigitte Bardot Paris also

gorgeous also nude the changes made
by each action are equal not
in velocity but in the impact
of bodies illuminating the night sky
unexpected blooming with fireworks and trails
of gunpowder metallic particles inhaled [PART

SIXTH] velocities in contrary directions are
reciprocally proportional this law takes place
also in attractions as in the
very small way the moon is
always falling towards the Earth in
my last dream of Hadley he

sleeps in a field I hold
a mirror to his mouth to
see if he's still breathing I
can't anymore touch him feel him
mirror angled to the sun catching
fire wind husking the field up

to an uncontrollable burn in perhaps
the oddest adaptation Ivo Saliger's 1939
painting shows Paris costumed as a
member of the Hitler Youth dark
brown uniform shorts and shirt he
sits on a rock underneath a

tree choosing between three robust naked
Aryan women drab brown and olive
green landscape unfolding behind them in
a promotional shot the starlet stands
a lone negligent waif on the
pier balancing on the bottom rung

of the railing shoes kicked to
the side she bends slightly away
from us towards the sea wind
tossing back her messy voluptuous tresses
the questions never fail to take
me by surprise in the middle

of a script I've already learned
I'm saying *it's often the case*
that the weight of an object
remains even after that object has
been released for the relinquishing of
objects does not necessarily secure peace

So press this fire to me

"The body is not a thing, it is a situation: it is our grasp on
the world and our sketch of our project."

Simone de Beauvoir, *The Second Sex*

ONE

[PART FIRST] because only by breaking
the tide pool's reflection can starfish
and anemone appear I'll admit I
despise the word *muse* detest my
collapse into *the architect's wife* not
merely a matter of outside perception

but even his voice over the
phone I internalize until all that's
salvageable is some terrible decorative urn
I picture him leaning forehead to
window city below—*without you* he
repeats into my ear *my designs*

lack grace you have to come
back my mind exceedingly unclear we've
been separated for weeks and for
weeks I've lived beside the Black
Sea wrapped in nostalgia for the
Russian Riviera of my mother's Soviet

youth another figment not mine held
tight I reverberate with hotel sounds
rough sheets red message light punctuating
sleep with a desire to become
a folktale Firebird my own fortune
and downfall plumage erupting into bonfire's

turbulent flame [PART SECOND] when did
I adopt the plunging neckline of
a gala dress his habit of
stopping me mid-sentence to grab his
notebook write furiously no longer flatters
me the interviews where he says

if not for my wife my
degeneration into cliché not the fault
of Barbie or Disney it's the
twenty-first century no kids to blame
perhaps I identify with objects too
much gaze out the window too

long repeating the word *bird* until
people places events entire networks go
a-shiver and instead of embracing this
blur dear reader I've always been
afraid as when birds develop new
feathers blood circulates up the shaft

creating a vulnerable state even gentle
handling accidental bumping into toy or
cage causes pain and if a
blood feather breaks you must pull
it immediately stop the bleeding heal
the wound phone clamped to my

ear he seems unable to stop
talking *building and landscape are continuous*
phenomena for instance in Iran the

Arg-é Bam pre-Islamic citadel composed of
narrow winding streets high adobe walls
roofed at intervals calcified into a

shell against invasions of rival tribes
and expansive sands and as he
talks I picture our studio apartment
white cube stark window dominated by
the Queensboro Bridge cantilever skyline traffic
photograph his voice syllables bouncing off

satellites moving like wind between building
A and B into the courtyard's
exposed space now tell me when
a self becomes air does it
echo or just vanish in all
versions of the story the Firebird's

feathers never cease glowing just one
feather lights the large room where
I sleep as if submerged in
water outside dark converging with inside
deep [PART THIRD] when I sleep
alone I sleep as if tidal

even when I wake I move
in the manner of an empty
boardwalk snow covered palms overtaken by
a sudden wave nature won't render
the bird entirely vulnerable for blood
feathers have larger quills than mature

feathers and begin protected by a
waxy sheath my mother's version of
the tale starred Maryushka an orphan
girl famous in her village for
embroidering into silks sun chariots hot
to the touch leopards you can

hear softly breathing as she embroiders
her own fate she herself becomes
the Firebird transformed by the Tsar
she would not obey my deepest
memories take place on a béton
brut balcony wool blanket bare skin

might I construct a little theater
of language to understand what happens
when the architect transforms my philosophies
into structures my fantasies into rooms
this I wouldn't begrudge him believe
me this isn't simply about envy

when I enter his blueprints I
empty into a replica of the
architect's wife [PART FOURTH] while the
husband referred to across texts as
master as *genius* as *star* fuses
with concrete steel and glass I

become thought dispersed or else I
cower in the corner a dog
afraid of being kicked unable to

sleep past dawn I slip into
the empty ballroom play the piano
entranced by its sound so terribly

warped by proximity to the sea
in my ragged wallet photograph we
recline under a blue shade sail
reader this is the truth it
was my idea to collaborate joining
to my vision his design *let's*

make you a starchitect I said
half-laughing half-serious pulling him to me
let's create a genius patrons will
line up to hire but when
the feather matures the blood supply
recedes now the feather might be

broken without consequence he says over
the phone *shifting elements beg to*
be conquered by concrete steel and
glass in my mother's version the
Tsar transforms himself into an enormous
raptor and carries the Firebird off

but rather than submit she sheds
feather after feather floating down on
meadow and forest and field and
of course this results in her
death his lands burning away beneath
them [PART FIFTH] Maria Tallchief heroine

of my youth the first famous
Native American ballerina she updated an
art musty with origins in Renaissance
amusement for European nobility and embraced
New York City Ballet mistress Bronislava
Nijinska's philosophy of discipline when you

sleep sleep like a ballerina even
on the street waiting for a
bus you must stand like a
ballerina Tallchief's 1949 performance of George
Balanchine's *Firebird* made her a legendary
instance of beauty's power to transcend

bigotry the theater of language succeeding
only when each *I* each *not-I*
is felt vividly *the cathedral is
a badly stated problem* he says
into my ear he says to
nobody in particular *you must help*

us solve this as I think
of our apartment our bed kitchenette
Japanese screen in front of the
toilet for modesty we do okay
but there's never enough money adult
birds typically replace all their feathers

during a molt the loss staggered
over several months ensures enough feathers
for insulation and flight but also

creates continual risk of blood feathers
broken on the balcony as wind
rushes the courtyard and packet boats

pull their moorings [PART SIXTH] according
to previous sensibilities the sky was
imprinted with volumes of untranslatable text
enticing readers to give themselves over
to the invisibility of wind for
if we consider true qualities indispensable

to their objects to what object
has molting become necessity to what
woman the name wife what town
Tsarist palaces politburo dachas crumbling Soviet
sanitariums because Maria Tallchief while still
operating within ballet's essential structure didn't

perform the Firebird as general dancer
but became the Firebird deepening self
into art and animal some wild
birds such as goldfinch molt annually
changing to bright plumage during breeding
season captivated by transformation we rarely

recognize underlying risk having first appeared
in the narrative as a good
loyal dog I find myself still
begging for scraps even as I
ironic wear with my dinner dress
a rhinestone-studded collar a more polite

illustration we can find in the
marble spa salon where Chekhovian aristocrats
once took curative baths this persists
under the public banya of workers
and peasants now converted into the
Novye Russkie's afterhours bathhouse dear reader

I too despise this next admission:
we had been parted for weeks
and for weeks I wore his
robe not for its satin sheen
but for its weight holding me
to the bottom of the sea

TWO

[PART FIRST] in the philosophical thought
experiment known as "Mary's Room" a
woman is imprisoned from birth in
a black and white room not
only are her walls painted black
and white but her skin hair

blood clothes furniture food by tricks
of theatrical lighting all appear to
her black and white on the
back of a photograph of Yalta's
promenade I write "Earth was early
in its forming when a planetesimal

careened into it resulting in catastrophic
crash" last summer my sister suggested
I work with a designer create
a chic line of dishes pillows
and curtains patterned floral over geometric
delicacy I responded with a vague

smile my most useful invention moving
like wind along passageways telling the
Slavic tale of rusalki spirits of
girls who died violently before their
time figured as fish-women living beneath
rivers and in the middle of

the night they walk out to
the banks dance and sing mesmerize
handsome young men coax them into
water to drown I understand this
because once in near-dark I found
a white-throated sparrow with the most

beautiful face [PART SECOND] when I
feel I feel the abdomen-pull of
a sparrow battering around in a
bush never having experienced color Mary
craves knowledge of color nevertheless and
from black-and-white books she learns about

optics the eye's structural connection to
neural processing from black-and-white videos she
learns specular reflection and scattering fierce
rulers of the Earth and all
its inhabitants rusalki ride upon clouds
in the form of birds directing

rain called *milk from heaven fertilizing
fields* on the back of a
photograph of the seaside bandstand I
write "the planet fragment moved with
such force it was destroyed when
it crashed into still-forming Earth" my

concept of architecture as conduit for
intensity passing from body to body
human animal inanimate material but how

does the architect do more than
merely stage this [PART THIRD] it's
not that I disdain design for

example Charlotte Perriand's B306 chaise longue
1928 streamlined chrome bent tubular steel
and leather cushioning inspired by the
sinuous lines of 18th-century day beds
cradling the body the sparrow after
struggling against the bush its damaged

wing trailing from the nape of
my neck to the base of
my spine feathering language into fire
the song bird's modesty undone on
the radio Mary listens to descriptions
of phosphorous tides and sunset's green

flash studying all day she acquires
an unrivaled body of knowledge and
without ever having gone outside she
writes books about the physical aspects
of color a set of works
we must proclaim from a scientific

point of view marvelously complete on
the back of a photograph of
the lobby's chandelier I write "the
molten core of an alien fragment
dissolves into and thus transforms the
elemental nature of Earth" imagine an

architecture that transcends its own theory
to become a relationship between bodies
much deeper than conscious knowing and
therefore moving beyond *pravda* truth in
righteousness and law to *istina* truth
in innermost being described by Vladimir

Nabokov as a state that refuses
to rhyme with anything else when
angry at their worshippers rusalki comb
their hair harder and harder creating
not rain but floods they also
produce wind and like Artemis control

the phases of the moon [PART
FOURTH] in Ukraine rusalki associated with
moon maidens direct the sun's rays
woodcarvings show horses and great-maned lions
emerging from their bodies an architecture
encouraging a vision of the self

rising and falling with crests and
troughs on the back of the
photograph of driftwood propped in a
cross I write "damage tons of
rock flung into orbit more than
sand and salt he tastes like

this" or consider Lily Reich's Bauhaus
designs even her quick sketches of
chairs the Barcelona and Brno simple

curved lines and exceptional balance usually
attributed to Ludwig Mies van der
Rohe so elegant let us suppose

Mary's eventually released by her captors
what exactly philosophers wonder does she
discover as she steps into the
garden syllables coming up from her
stomach to circle her lungs plunge
through her heart and bellow out

her mouth mica flecks shimmering [PART
FIFTH] to say the world with
the language of headache's pain taste
of wine burnt sky the most
compelling identification of rusalki with celestial
fire however is Russia's beloved folktale

The Firebird how entrancing my great-grandfather's
magic lantern slides depicting young Tsarevich
Ivan bear-skin cape little red boots
the Firebird part-peacock part-ibis Mary exclaiming
to the rose so *that's what*
it is like to experience red

and that—standing on grass with
bare feet—*is what it is*
like to experience green the shadow
of jets in flight an arrow
mistaken for migrating geese or for
example Greta Magnusson Grossman's 1948 iconic

cobra lamp flexible neck hooded metal
shade now so ubiquitous we don't
consider the person who designed it
on the back of a photograph
of small stones that pass for
sand I write "consider the moon's

formation traces of calcium of aluminum
and magnesium indicate it was flung
from Earth at impact" will you
hold me in contempt when I
suggest replacing the building as machine
with architecture as extension of multiple

selves organic and inorganic living and
nonliving events atmospheres tones all a-ripple
between us are us [PART SIXTH]
what forms for being might we
construct from architecture as networked desire
on the back of a photograph

of cloudless sky I write "unlike
the moon other satellites created upon
impact only orbited Earth until the
gravitational pull of distant planets destabilized
the system enough to free them"
did this parting tear like my

hem caught on a rock when
I wandered so far I didn't
know if I could find my

way back I hear you in
the spaces between satellites and when
you rise from your chair I

move so close to the window
I can feel weather moving through
the Firebird linked to lunar phases
suggests the body's decomposition as the
self-devouring goddess moves from generation to
death and must from her own

ashes be continuously reborn into *svoboda*
the freedom of the steppe and
the rebel and into *volya* fists
full of burning petals glistening drops
but unlike Grossman Perriand Reich who
were technically trained and so intimate

with their materials I'm almost exclusively
concept and thought a little philosophical
story of experience gaped raw before
idea seals the wound of touch
and sight *I can no longer
tell* Mary says *whether or not*

I was reading or dreaming running
fingers over sandpaper the smell of
a skunk feel of sharp light
bright purple unfastening weather moves me
as if I were no more
than a sheet in afternoon breeze

THREE

[PART FIRST] according to Aristotle analogy
articulates not only corresponding structure but
also shared abstraction for instance the
saltiness of the sea explained by
the saltiness of sweat reveals every
growing thing leaves a residue like

something burnt I understand architecture to
work like this thus by designing
for the inner organism the house
becomes a shell becomes released into
spirit in this way modernist Eileen
Gray counters Le Corbusier's machine for

living and thinks into existence a
new mode of being I hadn't
taken my key to our apartment
and had to ring up nobody
answering although light illuminated the edge
of the curtain threshold home perhaps

because I find it so easy
to leave I'm fascinated by fidelity
to place for example Moscow set
alight again and again its citizens
discovering in the Firebird a story
compelling them to stay rising from

ashes each time more stately and
magnificent [PART SECOND] for the drama
for the tenacity I'd like to
claim if my city was burning
I would stand in the central
square hem of my dress smoldering

my hair catching fire analogous objects
share not only relation but also
texture and process for example note
the fluidity channeling blood is to
artery as water is to conduit
my sister saying over the phone

the moment I realized he was
gone I was at his desk
in his library surrounded by his
books in this self-same moment I
understood he had never been more
than a collection of texts Gray's

masterpiece she names E-1027 minimalist villa
built 1929 on the Côte d'Azur
a love nest a study of
sun and wind the intimacy of
windows allows while lounging in bed
a view of the sea I

paused in the foyer of our
building ringing up imagining him submerged
in a halo of lamplight absorbed

in blueprints his vodka and Stockhausen
his round Le Corbusier glasses so
predictable [PART THIRD] I would like

to tell you I'd stand proudly
burning with my burning city but
in truth I'd likely hitch a
ride out of town as the
invalids are airlifted from the hospital
the analogy parquet is made of

wood as mosaic is made of
glass takes into consideration the breaking
apart of one substance in order
to create patterning such as herringbone
basketweave a peacock in the center
border inlaid with Greek keys E-1027

meditates on water and light the
cupboards and storage units designed for
evening sun glittering over contents its
sunken solarium lined with iridescent tiles
staircase rising from the center of
the house an inner nautilus I

rang up nobody answered did he
watch me walk away overcoat fluttered
open to release the iron red
the anthem red the Crimean red
of my dress *imagine* my sister
said in a whisper *when I*

looked through his books and found
underlined his favorite little philosophies written
with the exact same phrases he
was given to suggesting he had
invented [PART FOURTH] *you might think*
Maryana she said *that I now*

had the full extent of the
man at my disposal but instead
the more I read of his
collection the more difficult it's become
to remember the weight of his
body the taste of his breath

yes I replied *the life of*
the mind often works like this
in another scenario I'm the one
inside and he's the one caught
in rain ringing up as I
sit at the table in my

long red dress its color moving
into me as I close my
eyes fire around my throat fire
at my wrists when Napoleon rode
through Moscow's empty streets rather than
allow him to take it the

Muscovites burnt their city down in
the case of the analogy rose
is to flower as sapphire is

to gem the terms *flower* and
gem are subject to whims of
association until *rose* calls into being

a mistake of silk and *sapphire*
viewed from the window of a
plane an ungraspable coast Gray moves
out after her relationship ends and
when Le Corbusier friend of her
ex-lover visits he's incensed by E-1027's

design so like his own white
cube horizontal lines *murals destroy architecture*
he writes then frescoes her walls
with women Picasso-style nudes in Riviera
heat he paints naked later builds
his famous *cabanon* overlooking E-1027 he

will drown in the sea beneath
them [PART FIFTH] during the second
World War the violence of the
villa's trajectory intensifies occupied by retreating
Germans used for target practice one
of its later owners a psychiatrist

and morphine addict is murdered in
its rooms E-1027 then abandoned to
squatters we would be wise to
keep in mind that when one
charts the stars one charts the
movement one has oneself made in

virtue of the Earth's rotation we
call this point of view scientific
fact and yet it's natural to
feel quite certain the stars themselves
are shifting and so suppose a
message instructing us to move as

needles knit as looms weave as
forests grove as trees arboretum as
analogy compresses into a mouthful of
earth a fist of petals and
unstrung pearls what is there to
say years later visiting the city

of my mother's birth its exterior
renovated to resemble a nostalgic version
of its former self and yet
there are bathtubs in each flat
a series of malls replacing factories
that used to stand beyond the

old ring road in another scenario
we are both home he sits
across the table from me I
wait for the room to cool
before opening my eyes [PART SIXTH]
the body requires the attention of

hands and so press this fire
to me collar and cuffs pearl
buttons down my spine in the

21st century the story uplifts and
E-1027 declared a landmark is returned
to Gray's vision although Le Corbusier's

murals also restored maintain the status
of national treasures protected works of
art and we must ask how
a house built for a life
of spirit could ever be satisfied
by casual museum visitors before returning

home I watched night stretch across
the old city to the new
city its block housing and skyscrapers
O Phoenixcity Firebirdcity a woman standing
at the window necklace glittering the
plunging neckline of her gala dress

as arboreta preserve trees groves become
forests weave on a loom knit
with needles I make a tapestry
of this I make a little
tune of pine rising salt in
the mouth gull in the ear

FOUR

[PART FIRST] to know oneself by
a winter red dress buttons up
the back an intentionally complicated *yes*
for is inner nature harbored by
our names take mine Maryana for
example Russian form of Miryam Hebrew

for Mary perhaps of Egyptian origin
derived from *mery meryt* translated as
beloved only daughter slipping between cultures
and syllables *the meaning of a*
house he said next to me
in bed through the dark *cannot*

exist beyond the intention of its
architect which in turn shapes the
nature of its inhabitants in counterpoint
I think of Denise Scott Brown's
embrace of the messy vitality of
American vernacular sprawl her and her

husband's structures attend to the attractions
and repulsions both social and physical
contextualizing place and just as we
first shelter in our mothers' bodies
later we wander searching for a
persona a narrative dwelling virtually unknown

in 1910 Igor Stravinsky composes for
the Ballet Russes his famous version
of *The Firebird* he doesn't tell
the story of a village girl
inordinately good at sewing there's no
flight over the city no watching

it burn no in your arms
as we fall to ash [PART
SECOND] we search for home within
the musicality of an enchanted garden
a prince named Ivan a spellbound
princess an exotic bird glittering discordant

against simplistic harmonies of Ivan now
hunting now capturing what I wonder
is it like to feel oneself
to be a body created for
hunting capturing imprinting with violets or
was it thumbs and lips our

selves fluid and multiple harbor structures
of thought other scholars insist my
name derives from a Hebrew compound
of *mer* bitter and *yam* sea
or *meri* and the suffix *am*
meaning their rebellion a bird cresting

wind crying *bird bird bird* the
same note hit in excess of
what creates the citadel the barracks

the armory *for example* he continued
through the dark *if I were*
to build for myself a house

with sides made entirely of glass
the floor of pine not flush
with the ground but to manufacture
the illusion of floating raised ten
inches above [PART THIRD] *I would*
he continued *perch this glass bird*

on the edge of a hillcrest
and create below a reflecting pool
lined with Egyptian turquoise initially cold
but then warming as the body
submerges in exchange for release the
Firebird offers a glowing feather by

this gesture does she mean to
merely pay her debt or does
she mean call me call me
please and I think of Jeanne
Gang's Aqua Tower, blue glass Chicago
skyscraper with sky gardens and undulating

concrete terraces creating stunning sightlines social
spaces a vertical landscape of hills
valleys pools confuses the wind and
directs birds away from flying headlong
into their own reflections to know
oneself a little slash of light

a little eyelet in the weave
of other translators breaking Miryam into
mor and *yam* myrrh of the
sea *mari* and *yam* mistress of
the sea *mar* and *yam* drop
of the sea float away marine

the body a dwelling blood organs
bones in skin in dress in
cities continents atmospheres [PART FOURTH] the
concept of home acknowledges identity is
by structure repeatedly determined and then
he paused and then said *for*

the interior I'd design open space
divided by low walnut cabinets Lucite
shelving a single brick cylinder containing
the bathroom for privacy although the
bed—the bed would be out
in the open and what might

we understand then night after night
sleeping in full view of the
weather in Rabbinic literature Miryam is
derived not from a compound of
mari and *yam* but from a
single word *merum* meaning bitterness bitter

one wings embedded in amber near
the lake the Firebird watches Ivan
hide behind a tree the captive

princess sleepwalking slips from her dress
to know the raw feel of
what-it-is-like just before I come into

this name *this* house *this* relation
rather than *that* this requires an
architecture in excess even of the
chapel the temple cathedral basilica and
mosque [PART FIFTH] in excess of
archive library gallery palace of fine

arts Lina Bo Bardi's São Paulo
museum red concrete beams and voluminous
glass box creates an open exhibition
space releasing visitors into an anti-hierarchical
field of paintings suspended on glass
panels they appear to float such

fluidity affords multiplicity of access this
exhibition system replaced in 1966 by
labyrinths of white walls *and imagine*
he said *if I were to*
also build a house for you
upon the crest opposite and echoing

the proportions of my glass house
but completely enclosed in brick a
purely interior dwelling warmed by thick
carpets a fire in the fireplace
casting stories over the dark in
the water's reflection the Firebird reads

the future and finds Ivan clutching
her glowing feather calling on her
to help him break the spell
that keeps the princess from him
an architecture with origins organic constructivist
palladian gothic brutalist practical translators consider

Miryam to be a simple noun
meaning *elpis* hope a connection produced
less by etymology than by narrative
for Moses' sister Miryam stands as
a symbol for hope [PART SIXTH]
perhaps the most inspired derivation finds

the first half of the name
in the Egyptian *mer* or *mar*
to love and the second half
in the Hebrew divine name *Yam*
or *Yaweh* thus joining lost tribe
to sphinx architecture like language creates

such passageways Zaha Hadid's Middle East
Center for Oxford University a smooth
curving form stainless steel cladding the
building bends making way for a
century-old sequoia tree façade reflecting sky
and the campus' Victorian structures interior

punctuated by teardrop skylights houses document
and photograph archives workspace auditorium the
building sweeps up to a square

glass façade confronting or opening to
1970s Brutalist architecture upon waking from
enchantment Ivan and the princess embrace

delighted to find themselves no longer
prince and princess but peasants interwoven
with land at their country wedding
the Firebird transformed into an ordinary
songbird watches from a wickerwork cage
architecture manifests patterns of dwelling patterns

of being patterns of thought *we
would discover* he softly said taking
my hand *although my house embodies
revelation when we look to the
reflecting pool we would see it
completely subsumed by the impenetrability of*

your brick to know oneself the
over-pink rose caught in a sphere
of glass and so dew-tipped and
never-fade but what does it become
when you break it when you
break it out of the glass

LET US BE AS APERTURE

Homage for Maya Deren

"Every fabric is initially the result of two elements:
the character of the fibers used in the thread construction—
that is, the building material—and the construction,
or weave, itself."

ANNI ALBERS, "Interrelation of Fiber and Construction"

ONE

[PART FIRST] in our only collaboration
I play a heroine possessed by
spirits during the siege of Dubrovnik
in the first scene I hear
music nobody else can hear drawing
me down concrete stairs to a

pebbled beach flanked by limestone fortresses
fig tree bluffs Adriatic opening and
I float a montage with views
of the Gate of Pila the
Gate of Ploča our creative project
forms in slow water with shale

deposits found in lakes and lagoon
sediment and in river deltas along
floodplains we ask what is the
intrinsic nature of black-and-white film in
her 1947 essay "Creative Cutting" Maya
Deren instructs that if the duration

of a shot exceeds the duration
of an action there's a decrease
in tension thus Hesiod promises love's
scarf protects the pulse at the
throat gulls banking gulls plummeting in
and out the spotlight our script

a collection of diagrams old letters
and news clips as we shift
from the self-as-object to the self-as-process
exterior entwines with history interior becomes
a desert film of uninhabitable regions
where sand storms articulate the psyche

because to perform a woman possessed
is to transform into a woman
possessed [PART SECOND] at each return
hold the camera in stillness registering
the inevitable shift of dunes effacing
wind-lines animal tracks this is my

material interior filmed at the height
of the sternum six inches from
the chest during the month of
extreme convulsion we speak of snow
in the past tense which does
nothing to lessen the duration of

April on heavier days I sink
into the sorrel pasture's dank coat
finding creative vision in shale deposited
on the continental shelf in deep
quiet water a process taking millions
of years as when you walk

into the room you let the
breeze in gulls alternating the spotlight
set to the spider-lace scarf edging

hands' low distraction Hesiod says *love*
if it is love performs loosening
and for this reason Deren writes

"a static shot of a building
becomes boring if held longer than
identification or appreciation requires" the camera
dictating descend the stairs nouning *erosion*
rebar sand the interior a desert
of glass not until reviewing the

footage did I realize you filmed
me that morning half-naked wandering through
sea holly and stonecrop to graffitied
ruins of the Hotel Belvedere de
Luxe Dubrovnik seventeen stories of abandoned
sand-colored stone cascading from cliff to

sea [PART THIRD] on off days
securing shutters against the city center
I spend afternoons in bed watching
YouTube videos of missiles launched into
the Fortress of the Passing Bell
into boats moored at the Old

Port while outside sun blares across
limestone walls and tourists here in
the midst of Adriatic floating I
discover filming the desert as the
always present absence in the middle
of a crowded room given a

static shot of something for example
a cliff skyscraper horizon we know
lasts longer than the duration of
the shot we feel nothing critical
will happen to the object after
it leaves our field of vision

consequently such camerawork creates in relation
to reality no tension wind gusting
through an empty ballroom's chandelier Hesiod
says *but do not forget love*
says *the field extending under gulls*
angling the spotlight set to the

heroic scarf brought to the lips
this is creation as fissility and
we are shale splitting easily along
the bedding plane into small thin-lipped
fragments with rust stains from exposure
of pyrite to air blooming yellow

efflorescent sulfur and so yes now
split and now blossom [PART FOURTH]
in equating creative process with landscape
undergoing rupture we prepare to undergo
the permeability of shale increased by
force of fracturing fluid injecting water

sand and chemicals into sealed-off portions
of the borehole on the nightstand
two forms of history: a black-and-white

photograph featuring a limestone statue of
Dubrovnik's patron protector of independence Saint
Blaise a model city cradled in

his outstretched hands this framed next
to an artist's rendering of the
Hotel Belvedere de Luxe the angularity
of '80s architecture softened by pastel's
expressive gestures and *de luxe* in
floriated script sleepless I focus on

these images overridden by gulls ascending
gulls wheeling spotlight set to abstract
the Hesiod scarf worrying lungs' low
breath loosening limbs of love interior
syntax cutting crescents over dunes as
black-and-white film deepens our pleasure taken

in the relation of illusion to
optics what if we are all
just avoiding a natural state of
uncertainty the very last sequence of
Deren's short dance film *A Study
in Choreography for Camera* provides an

example of the use of duration
as tension the dancer taking off
from the ground for a leap
the shot cutting out while his
body continues ascending the frame [PART
FIFTH] this followed by a single

slow shot against sky legs travelling
horizontally the plateau of his leap
followed by a shot in which
he moves descendingly through the frame
to land with such softness in
contrast the force of applied pressure

causes the formation to fracture fracturing
fluid fissuring rock releasing natural gas
petroleum brine and what if we
are not objects but more properly
acts of relation our own apparent
boundaries a point of view created

by static forms imposed on dynamic
systems such as the sensation of
entering a darkened room its contours
subsumed by sandalwood and leather deep
in the ruins of the bombed-out
hotel I found history unbroken china

embossed with the hotel's logo packs
of notepaper still sealed in cellophane
receipts calculated in the Yugoslav dinar
alone in the ruins I say
porušen pokvaren slomljen speaking a language
I never learned star dune seif

dune running parallel to wind over
contours of sand gulls plying gulls
whittling over spotlights set to love

the Hesiod scarf drawing a low
musical horizon first electrified then gone
dim I am perhaps too good

at playing someone else's heroine and
this failure rather than some form
of desire often propels my own
films [PART SIXTH] gulls over sea
over fields low banking the coastal
scarf a Hesiod wind a soul

let loose in spotlight as the
throat reveals the heart's low throb
Deren's *Study in Choreography* has the
quality of slow floating yet creates
more tension than any other sequence
in her films for the leap

endures much longer than in actuality
it would and she allows no
single shot to satisfy the normal
necessity of gravity our most inventive
scene was a compromise filmed quickly
on the ferry to Hvar I

take a compact from my purse
wind unscarving my hair I peer
into the reflection my face replaced
by desert dunes a crescent moon
hung at the edge of a
white sky solid proppant usually sand

added to fracture fluid keeps the
fracture open even after injections stop
this creates flowback water requiring offsite
treatment for brine hydrocarbons metals and
radioactivity through a bombed-out hole in
the ballroom I emerge before an

empty pool tiled Adriatic blue cornflowers
and lavender endangered push through cracks
salt and seed wanting the building
back as the self unfolds in
twenty-four frames per second a species
of illusion but what is truth

TWO

[PART FIRST] "the aesthetic problem of
form exists essentially and simultaneously as
a moral problem" writes Deren in
An Anagram of Ideas on Art
and so how to perform an
ethical relation to the footage of

a flood mobile homes uprooted a
man in a canoe paddling after
his lowing cow the film then
cutting to the tremor of a
hand-held camera actress gagged and bound
to the bed how to punctuate

but not erase such images with
the reminder that destruction's a cause
for coming into being and we
are all born of a fusion
of cells necessarily dissolving each individual
cell's unity the window of experience

thereby opening as narrative drops away
like a rocket disintegrating in the
atmosphere after placing its small payload
in orbit thus desire overtakes fidelity
to particular identity creating forms woven
with process and event for example

the house-fire conveyed by a paper
model hung in a tree then
match-flick lit conflagration fanned by wind
transiting across branches [PART SECOND] as
a tornado takes on the substance
of its surroundings film accumulates landscapes

and objects according to its art
damask dress damask curtains damask couch
emotional impact deriving not from what
we see but materializing as a
complex of images humming in our
ears as we enter the scene

through an aerial shot roof torn
off the film invites us to
equate the house with a dollhouse
actress with doll but then the
camera zooms in silk gag filling
the screen a dark patch where

breath seeps in and out the
taste of wet fabric purple dye
in your mouth window opening as
each fact of your narrative detaches
from its original setting and begins
revolution around another fact as answer

to the aesthetics the ethics of
relation found in choosing always the
more violent word so that the

text of the world and the
text of the work are stitched
through with the same salt-infusing vision

the sensate skin of the real
felt along the unfurled edges of
a lily where pollen dust recalls
fire that edged but never entered
our garden [PART THIRD] to be
as wind through a chandelier rustling

burn the ragged muslin edge of
the curtains and the dress this
prevents unraveling who else will take
such care with the finishing of
a shroud to feel the edge
of life continuing into death you

ride with rebels deep into the
desert and say nothing as you're
pressed by one of them face-first
into sand his body on top
of your body as shots fire
out the interior casting camera as

hero you are not only a
self and splinter as you run
still filming into the center of
a sandstorm again and again as
someone props open the window and
facets of your narrative now circle

each other in a system of
multiple stars and the plot points
of your life become both autonomous
and irrevocably coalesced camera swooning from
chandelier to gagged breath from objective
to subjective shots we play God-as-spider

losing his neutrality God-as-spider falling into
the world and so subsequent sequences
become shaded with divine justice *but
do you* he asks adjusting the
scarf tied around my neck *do
you deserve a spectator's intervention* [PART

FOURTH] streamed live online the crowd
pours onto the street chanting and
effigies flags lighter fluid match pushed
back by taser and club the
camera steady on a fallen woman
then the screen goes black we

who hold our little acts of
consciousness like a lover's letter folded
and refolded to an inner pocket
we should well be anxious lest
our gestures trace the poachers' use
of song bird recordings to lure

sparrows into nets someone opens the
window and each star in the
multiple-star system that once had been

your narrative now attracts other orbiting
bodies and those orbiting bodies as
you watch begin to attract other

bodies the camera's complexity creating at
times the illusion of being itself
almost a living intelligence you stand
at the threshold processing the room
at a Dutch tilt how does
the camera differ from the fleur-de-lis

branding the red heifer marking her
animus revertendi from *ferae naturae* which
is just a pretty way of
saying *I domesticate you* [PART FIFTH]
in the 1936 recording of Pablo
Casals playing Bach's *Six Suites for*

Unaccompanied Cello we hear three forms
of breath Casals breathing the instrument
breathing the composition breathing as you
sit there becoming lens and film
a sound-form deep in the throat
coming out of the mouth's soft

O a mode of language brought
on by uncertainty are you a
dark sea culminating in a darker
horizon where Deren writes "if form
in art comprehends moral form no
one who presumes to address profound

human values in their art is
exonerated from responsibility for the negative
actions of their failures and errors"
documentary techniques establish what can be
said of the exterior while metaphor
and juxtaposition articulate interior fact his

ribs mouth pulse palm filmed as
ecstasy splinters in her hair dust
in her mouth this happens at
twenty-four frames per second a woman
and a man becoming dissolution as
someone opens the window and in

comes music from what you first
believe to be the eerie and
uncertain sounds of a glass harmonica
until you realize that what you're
hearing is the sound of the
star cluster that once had been

your narrative [PART SIXTH] the window
opens and you think *I am*
somewhere west of the Pleiades by
now and then you think of
a name that names no thing
the psyche-interior a process we like

to believe we comprehend but ultimately
ungraspable it folds into a desire
to harbor the fact and nature

of creation thus placing the camera
in the position Walter Benjamin ascribes
to Paul Klee's *Angelus Novus* while

we perceive a chain of events
the film reveals one single catastrophe's
continuous wreckage and so we must
respect the responsibility of transcending mere
record for in some cases a
representation transforms the original to such

a degree that the copy alters
what's real writing her *Anagram* just
after World War II Deren insists:
"surely the vacant eyes and desolated
bodies of starved children deserve and
require in the moral sense something

more than the maudlin clichés of
the tourist camera or the skillful
manipulations of a craftsman who brings
to them techniques developed for and
suitable to the entertaining demonstrations of
the manufacture of a Ford car"

THREE

[PART FIRST] let us convey our
heroine as beauty mouthing history into
the lens her future inscribed by
the ankh tattooed at the small
of her back her past a
grainy YouTube video of the Siege

of Dubrovnik followed by an iPhone
video of the shelling of eastern
Ukraine a distinctive film form Deren's
work suggests consists not in eliminating
the quotidian the natural the artifice
of other arts but in relating

these according to the special capacity
of film a night's worth of
time-lapse footage of the city under
siege illuminated by parachute flares spliced
with a clip of a folklorist
lecturing on the medieval tradition of

each May planting a Mary garden
its forget-me-nots a direct expression of
her eyes the maidenhair fern her
hair the cinquefoil rooted in her
five fingers and so touch the
tender yellow petals touch your lips

to lens beginning a film of
the interior with an unobstructed shot
of sky the camera zooms in
on our heroine's hands she selects
a bone-handled knife and over the
painted teardrops of tragedy's mask she

carves a deep flame [PART SECOND]
mask in hand our heroine pauses
as if harboring a matinee-length strand
of pearls in her belly and
so stands at the window lips
sealed against the adder pressing at

the back of her mouth stillness
pouring memory into the camera not
merely to reconstruct or measure the
original chronology of a life but
to place in immediate temporal sequence
events actually distant in time the

screen split between a charge of
antelopes through the hillside's satellite dishes
on the right-hand side while on
the left a documentary on early
mortars iron bowls reminiscent of kitchen
and apothecary vessels from which they

draw their name as thunderheads amass
and relinquish amass and clear we
film the self as weather transforming

the body's relationship to both abstract
and concrete objects of thought and
so let us regard the morning

glory of her skirt her baby's
breath scarf the Canterbury bells of
her hat [PART THIRD] an instance
of *smoke* indicates fire the word
here refers to place of utterance
now points to this very moment

unfolding before us are we wrong
to suppose the mask pleased to
bear in place of a predictable
emblem of grief a release of
light and heat the sting of
the knife an expression of relief

we film the sky from multiple
angles then recompose the sequence to
evoke sensations of wind gusting through
the limestone fortress while I listen
to the sound of a motorboat
subsuming the breath of the body

next to me "nothing can be
achieved in the art of film"
Deren writes "until its form is
understood to be the product of
a completely unique complex" the exercise
of an instrument that functions simultaneously

as discovery and invention as when
the stillness inside your favorite word
comes over you filling your body
with the pressure of air stopped
in the curves of a trombone
[PART FOURTH] if the filmmaker attempts

to convey an expression of floating
while herself submitting to gravity she
reveals a logic akin to the
making of a pearl for such
expressions require a catalyst as modest
as sand an observation as mundane

as patience amidst passing time the
potential of indexicality to wed abstraction
to the concrete is created perhaps
by the mind's relation to the
body and so let us call
this form of creation *the soul*

attending violets as blooms of humility
require humility the lily a queenship
the veronica an expression of faith
a complexity of the camera transforming
you from one who has been
marked by tragedy to an agent

who marks the world with tragedy
creating an audience with as much
empathy for Hera as for Medea

for Helen as for Penelope destruction
and beauty filling your mouth with
the dirt-gasp of abjection and awe

for such conditions are part and
parcel of accessing moments of silence
holding the center even as you
find yourself in the middle of
an explosion lifting the mask to
your face as the building across

the street uproots from its foundations
and flings itself into air [PART
FIFTH] within a film panning over
the jigsaw of clean sandstone reconstructing
a balustrade broken by a blast
is a film of a woman

setting fire to houses forests fields
shocked-up to ash floating down from
a vaulted ceiling fortress sinking tide
rising beauty employing the camera as
an opposing form like a hawk
narrows down to its prey the

indexical sign equivalent to a fragment
torn from its object the lily
of the valley with its nodding
flowers for example torn from the
base of the cross for at
the base of the cross you

tore out a lock of your
hair with a shift in context
the mask's teardrop becomes a symbol
for specific loss a time before
fire when we weightless floated under
the protection of the Fortress of

the Passing Bell the form proper
to film accomplished only by relating
its elements according to the special
time-based characteristics of both camera and
editing such that the reality created
is felt by the viewer through

and through [PART SIXTH] in *Meshes
of the Afternoon* Deren—who was
known to consult fortune-tellers not for
predictions of the future but for
readings of the present creates multiple
eye-line matches and mismatches employing extreme

angles implying a spider's point of
view looking down on Deren herself
playing a dreamer then cutting to
a reverse shot from the point
of view of a sleeping figure
after we ceased to believe in

mythologies of protection the teardrop was
taken for the lost earring of
a careless heiress a freshwater pearl

a misshapen bead fallen from some
monk's mala thus the symbol held
slightly ajar ushers the passage of

time weather and translation's movement from
the possession of a language to
the performance of a language our
heroine inhabits a role wherein half
the script has always been missing
to find oneself inside such conditions

is to stitch one's life to
the world by augury pointing and
singing a slow walk down a
path lined with bitter sorrow the
hosta blooming at the time of
the assumption fig trees marking the

way for a flight into Egypt
and so inhale the August lilies
grown atop the rampart paper house
folded into your pocket like a
lover's letter as the camera zooms
through the eye-slits of your mask

FOUR

[PART FIRST] in 1947 Deren disembarked
in Haiti on a Guggenheim grant
for an eight-month stay to film
ritual dance which she intended to
montage with hopscotch and other nonnative
movement four years and three trips

later 20,000 feet of unedited film
lay spooled in Deren's closet protected
by a fireproof box the psyche-interior
articulated by long shots of the
winded sea the metallic sea a
boat adrift red sails unfurled then

slackening becomes a question of ethics
and materiality in the 1960s four
oil islands are built in San
Pedro Bay off Southern California's coast
tapping into the third largest oil
field in the United States by

2002 ninety percent of the original
resource had been exhausted but even
if we hold ourselves in a
state of unknowing the soul during
sleep at times glances or even
peers intently at truth at light

striking images onto film wherein the
body becomes a rose now blossoming
now withering [PART SECOND] the soul
reading itself into syntax becomes a
carrier pigeon returning home after the
siege alighting on rubble nobody to

unstrap the message from its back
in the interior film waves break
around ankles the low long gesture
of hands describe fracture casting time
onto a sundial although the film
plays silently by the shape of

her mouth we know she is
saying something soft to someone outside
the frame in lieu of editing
her footage into a film Deren
writes *Divine Horsemen: The Living Gods
of Haiti* explaining she had begun

with the intent to turn elements
of a reality into art but
found herself compelled to abandon artistic
manipulation and record as transparently as
possible logics of movement and ritual
the soul gazing from the other

side of sleep sees a million
cubic yards of silt and sand
dredged from the bottom of the

harbor to create the islands' cores
providing a naturalistic finish large rocks
and boulders quarried at Catalina shipped

inland line their shores [PART THIRD]
faux skyscraper façades designed by Joseph
Linesch architect of Disney's Tomorrowland conceal
wellheads pipelines oil derricks consider this
in counterpose to a fidelity to
materiality that admits to the tornado

devastating a path from desert to
the sea undone in sand in
salt to mouth to eye to
skin Penelope's discourse on dreams given
in book nineteen of the *Odyssey*
leads us to understand that if

dream's veil permits the attentive soul
to perceive truth then the gates
of sleep are made of horn
which becomes transparent when thinned along
the shore of red sand mixed
with driftwood and burnt negatives where

I search the interior and find
smoke and flocks of doves pluming
up countless times Deren submitted
her footage for anthropological use but
an outsider to the field she was
ignored this she considered one of

her most significant failures [PART FOURTH]
the lacework of rose leaves denote
aphids silhouetted against a limestone wall
a woman bends trimming an errant
hedge becoming part-blade part-wrist we must
learn to read such shadows at

night multicolored spotlights bathe the oil
islands' façades and waterfalls dampen down
the drilling sound eleven years after
her death Anthology Film Archives received
five cartons of Deren's Haitian films
the physical condition of the footage

due to aging a state of
deterioration shrinkage darkness faded tonal quality
the soul captured to film manifests
as a woman checking her hair
in a windowed reflection spliced with
footage of fishing nets hauled into

a boat the interior composed of
quick cuts back and forth when
the veil of dream dulls vision
and prevents us from accessing truth
the gates of sleep are thought
to be made of ivory in

composition so dense that regardless of
dawn and the thinning will of
time they remain entirely opaque [PART

FIFTH] given the material natures of
horn and ivory we shouldn't be
surprised when Penelope tells us dreams

issued through the Gate of Ivory
delude us with promises never fulfilled
but dreams emerging from the Gate
of Horn are prophetic however translation
fails to disclose Penelope's play upon
the words κέρας horn and κραίνω

fulfill and upon ἐλέφας ivory and
ἐλεφαίρομαι deceive the material similarity of
word-forms stitching image to concept Deren's
films express the intrinsic nature of
a storm breaking over the bow
of the boat while in the

cabin twinned figures play chess as
herons grebes falcons parrots shelter in
the hundreds of palms planted to
stabilize the islands' soil with their
roots if the soul exists between
two people let us be as

aperture a six-second shot of sand
on salt-damp skin in 1973 Cherel
Winnett Ito and Deren's former husband
Teiji Ito edit Deren's footage although
the project had been advised against
archivists insisting that handling the fragile

film would jeopardize the only existing
copy [PART SIXTH] released in 1977
the Ito compilation of Deren's film
Divine Horsemen ironically was and is
still considered by many anthropologists to
be a classic study of Haitian

Voudoun while the Ito version manipulates
some of the material for example
the sound of birds chirping or
wings fluttering synchronized to images the
primary emphasis honors Deren's desire for
accurate conveyance of ritual with a

focus on dance through the Gate
of Horn the wind catches by
surprise four passersby on a little
bridge one turns to watch her
scarf blow sky-high alongside an arabesque
of papers torn from the hands

of another in a lecture for
the young women of Smith College
Deren compares the female artist to
Erzulie the Haitian goddess of love
feminine force muse of the arts
divinity of what unlike sex is

not essential to propagation but encompasses
everything beyond that which is necessary
for basic survival hidden behind a

fringe of palms and banana trees
hibiscus impatiens men and women in
hardhats forklift heavy pipes while a

technician in a trailer studies a
video monitor the picture of oil
extraction supplied by a tiny camera
5200 feet beneath the surface her
silhouette grows large as she lifts
a poppy to the sky forming

a conduit between materials animate and
inanimate organic and inorganic the source
of being and art a dissolution
felt first in the gut then
following out past the body in
a chain of image and syllable

NOTE

Blood Feather began over a decade ago as a six-sentence dramatic monologue. Although the words came from me, the voice of the fragment was foreign—*In autumn I decided / to cancel desire.* This persona glimmered enticingly, and I was drawn to unleashing her story—*I / fly in my sequined dress my / suit of lights*—while also wondering over the cultural and social forces propelling her script. To investigate this question and coax her into further speech, I took each sentence from the monologue and located a potential thread of cultural or personal narrative. I then spun these threads from research and imagination and wove them together to create the initial poem of what would become *Blood Feather*.

Both addicting and catalytic, this process generated the book's fabric: three long poems each spoken by a different female persona. From these women and the archives out of which they are created come facts and experiences resonant with the contemporary moment. For example: a 215 BCE Roman law forbade women to own more than an ounce of gold, ride in carriages, wear multicolored garments—particularly those trimmed in purple, symbolically male and royal. For example: incensed at the similarity between the architecture of his female contemporary Eileen Gray and his own structures, Le Corbusier frescoed the walls of her masterwork with

Picasso-style nudes. Having famously written that murals destroy architecture, his embellishment was no compliment.

We each experience life as an individual—a flesh and blood *I*—yes, and yet at the same time we are constructed out of archives and gestures already given. As the sister of one of the narrators tells her over the phone: *in his library surrounded by his / books ... I / understood he had never been more / than a collection of texts.* These structures shape the book's personae as they confirm and resist, collude with and attempt to reinvent, the cultural and personal histories that surround them.

Sources

Three sprigs of rosemary bound with red thread

Aristotle. *On the Generation of Animals.*

Bausch, Pina. *Kontakthof.*

Beck, Julian. 1972 "Acting Exercises: Notes for a Primary Lesson (1)," *The Life of the Theatre: The Relation of the Artist to the Struggle of the People.*

Brody, Richard. *Everything Is Cinema: The Working Life of Jean-Luc Godard.*

Cheiro. *The Language of the Hand.*

de Beauvoir, Simone. *Brigitte Bardot and The Lolita Syndrome.*

Dali, Salvadore. *The Judgment of Paris.*

Elkins, James. *What is an Image?*

Foreman, Richard. *Performance Studies Reader.*

Gish, Lillian. *Broken Blossoms or The Yellow Man and the Girl.*

J. Paul Getty Museum. *Storage Jar with the Judgment of Paris.*

Le Prince, Louis. *Roundhay Garden Scene.* 1888.

Lhote, Adre. *The Judgment of Paris.*

Newton, Sir Isaac. *Principia Mathematica.*

Nietzsche, Friedrich. *Notes on the Eternal Recurrence.*

Ratcliffe, Ann. *Mysteries of Udolfo.*

Slaiger, Ivo. *The Judgment of Paris.*
Tolstoy, Leo. *Anna Karenina.*
Wagner, Richard. *Lohengrin.*
Wagner, Richard. *Tristan und Isolde.*
Williams, Tennessee. *The Glass Menagerie.*

Google searches for history of cosmetics, application of eye makeup, Cleopatra, Marie Antoinette, The Judgment of Paris, history of naming Los Angeles

So press this fire to me

Abramovic, Marina. *The Artist is Present.*
Bacon, Mardges. *Le Corbusier: An Atlas of Modern Land-scapes.*
Balanchine, George. *Firebird.*
Bohm, Svetlana. *Another Freedom.*
Bohm. Svetlana. *Nostalgia.*
Colomnia, Beatriz. "Battle Lines: E.1027." *The Sex of Architecture.* Ed. Diana Agrest, Patricia Conway, Leslie Kanes Weisman.
Gregg, Melissa and Gregory J Seigworth. *The Affect Theory Reader.*
Hesse, Mary. *Aristotle's Logic of Analogy.*
Hubbs, Joanna. *Mother Russia: The Feminine Myth in Russian Culture.*
Jackson, Frank. "Epiphenomenal Qualia."
Jackson, Frank. "What Mary Didn't Know."
Johnson, Philip. *Glass House.*
Le Corbusier. *Towards a New Architecture.*

Maas, Anthony. "The Name of Mary." *The Catholic Encyclopedia.*

Stravinsky, Igor. *Firebird.*

Tallchief, Maria. *Firebird.* New York City Ballet.

Whistler, James Abbott McNeill. *The Princess from the Land of Porcelain.*

Google searches for analogy, reference, qualia, blood feather, songbird, ibis, magic lanterns, The Magic Lantern Society, Arg-é Bam, Persian gardens, paradise etymology, The Ballet Russes

LET US BE AS APERTURE

Alÿs, Francis. "Tornado 2000-2010."

Benjamin, Walter. *Theses on the Philosophy of History.*

Casals, Pablo. *Bach's Six Suites for Unaccompanied Cello.*

Deren, Maya. *A Study in Choreography for Camera.*

Deren, Maya. *An Anagram of Ideas on Art, Form and Film. Essential Deren: Collected Writings on Film by Maya Deren.* Ed. Bruce R. McPherson.

Deren, Maya. *At Land.*

Deren, Maya. "Creative Cutting." *Essential Deren: Collected Writings on Film by Maya Deren.* Ed. Bruce R. McPherson.

Deren, Maya. *Divine Horsemen: The Living Gods of Haiti.*

Deren, Maya. *Divine Horsemen: The Living Gods of Haiti.* (Film) Ed. Cherel Ito and Teiji Ito.

Deren, Maya. *Meditation on Violence.*

Deren, Maya. *Meshes of the Afternoon.*

Deren, Maya. *Ritual in Transfigured Time.*

Hesiod. *The Theogeny.* Trans. Hugh G. Evelyn-White.

Klee, Paul. *Angelus Novus.*

Kudláček, Martina. Interview with Robert Gardner. *Bomb Magazine.*

Kudláček, Martina. *In the Mirror of Maya Deren.*

"Mary Gardens." www.fisheaters.com

Perry, John. "Indexicals and Demonstratives." *Companion to the Philosophy of Language.* Ed. Robert Hale and Crispin White.

Sullivan, Moira. "Maya Deren's Ethnographic Representation of Ritual and Myth in Haiti." *Maya Deren and the American Avant-Garde.* Ed. Bill Nichols.

Turim, Maureen. "The Ethics of Form." *Maya Deren and the American Avant-Garde.* Ed. Bill Nichols.

Wall, Jeff. *A Sudden Gust of Wind.*

Young, Michael. "The Casualties of War: The Hotel Belvedere in Dubrovnik Croatia." www.untappedcities.com

ACKNOWLEDGMENTS

Fragments of *Blood Feather* have appeared in *Colorado Review* and *The Denver Quarterly*: thank you to these editors for including them. Forrest Gander selected "Three sprigs of rosemary bound with red thread," then titled *Sestina LA* for the 2010 Poetry Society of America award for a poem on a philosophical theme. Thank you to Alan Gilbert, GC Waldrep, Forrest Gander, Donna Stonecipher, David St. John, Dan Beachy-Quick, Mary Szbyist, Mary Jo Bang, Elizabeth Zuba, and Kristina Marie Darling for invaluable advice and encouragement with this manuscript. Thank you to Ashley Lamb for the cover collage and on-going inspiration. Thank you to Ann Aspell, David Rossitter, and Jeffrey Levine for making a home for this book and bringing it into the world.

KARLA KELSEY is the author of four full-length collections of poetry and a collection of speculative essays, *Of Sphere* (Essay Press, 2017). Poems and prose have appeared in journals such as *Bomb, Fence, Conjunctions, New American Writing, The Boston Review, The Colorado Review, The Denver Quarterly, Verse,* and *Tupelo Quarterly*. Her critical essays on poetry, poetics, and pedagogy have appeared in anthologies and literary journals. From 2010-2017 she edited *The Constant Critic,* Fence Books' online journal of poetry reviews. With Aaron McCollough she currently co-publishes SplitLevel Texts, a press specializing in book-length hybrid genre projects. A recipient of a Fulbright Scholar Award, she is Professor of Creative Writing at Susquehanna University's Writers Institute.